Isolation

Thoughts and poems to help you get through quarantine with a little less stress, and a little more laughter.

Sivon Pichoto

For the people I love
those who believe in me
and those who always pushed me
to reach for my dreams.

Note from the Author:

Although this book makes light of the current reality of the world, I do not want to go on without acknowledging the real lives that are being lost by this terrible virus. These people are brothers, sisters, fathers, mothers, friends, coworkers, grandparents. Let's all continue to stay safe together and love each other from a distance.

Special Dedications

Thank you to the following people. Without you, the launch of this book would not have been possible:

Heather Nieves
Christy Cholerton
Phillip Collinge
Taylor Warne
Stephanie Spangler
Debra Jones
Lauryn Brown
Lynn Spangler
Natalie Lamparter
Kim Carroll
Jennifer Folkenroth
Erika Karp
Shelby Wildgust
Alicea Rastelli
Amanda Matz
Josh Pillay
Chris Coronato
Manouk Hovhannesian

The world is silenced.
Roads.
Businesses.
Hopes.
Dreams.
Your world is silenced.

You sit down to watch Netflix...

But you've already finished it.

Amazon.
The most needed service,
but also the most feared.
Cardboard.
Cardboard everywhere.

The not-so-tech-savy come out of their caves.
They're revealed for who they really are.
It's a scary time
to be online.

...

...

...

...now what?

Everyone over 25 joins TikTok.
Chaos ensues.
Gen Z cries.

Stuck between worlds
inside yourself
The self you hate
and the self you desire

Fear

Faith

A decision.

Morning
Breakfast
Distraction
Panic
Lunch
Netflix
Maybe Shower
Panic Again
Dinner
Meditate
Search for Purpose
Sleep

Disconnected.
But more connected than ever.
Facetime and phone calls.
Virtual happy hours.
Family time.
Leaning back in to love.

Brenda bought 20 packs of toilet paper.
Brenda's a bitch.
Who doesn't
care
about anyone
else.

Finally having enough time to
wake up
in the morning.
But not having anything else
to fill the time.

The simple joy of changing out of your
night pajamas
and into your
day pajamas.

Arguing with your significant other about
the correct way
to cook
literally everything.

Becoming acutely aware
that the next generation
will be homeschooled
by day drinkers.

Marijuana.
Finally recognized
as a legitimate
medicine.

Remember to shower.
Remember to shower.
Remember to shower.
Remember to shower.

Always wanting more time.
Finally having it.
But
Still
Giving in
To the nothingness.

Doing nothing.
Wanting everything.

Panic. **Panic. PANIC.**
Anxiety...anxiety.
Fear. **Fear. FEAR.**
Scarcity.
Lost Wages.
Love.

You're looking around
To see if anyone's there
Nope. Party for one.

Every commercial
suddenly talking about
contactless delivery
and taking care of you.

Uncertainty about the future.
How will our world be different?
Will we be afraid to get close to each other?
Will we be more conscious?
How will work change?
Home life?
Social norms?

Sitting in the same room.
as someone you love.
Do you simply exist
together
or engage
in meaningful conversation?

Encouraging New Hobbies.
Uncovering Creativity.
Leaning in to Self Discovery.
Finding Inner Peace in the Silence.

Today
What are you up to?
Nothing.

Tomorrow
What are you up to?
Nothing.

The Next Day
What are you up to?
Nothing much.

Hand sanitizer.
Gloves.
Masks.
Pajama Pants.
Fashion.

Some drink to get through
Some create
Some smoke to get through
Some explore
Some distract to get through
Some engage
But we're all left wanting more

Your self confidence taking a hit when you find out you're considered non-essential.

Seeing your friends after quarantine
and suddenly trying to remember
if they've always looked that way.

Dogs
looking like they were groomed
by Edward Scissorhands

Husbands
finally seeing what their wives
really look like
after the hair color fades

The world finally unites.
Together we stand strong.
Against the enemy.
Carole Baskin.

Social   Distancing

Deciding to finally write that book
you've always wanted to write.
But then giving in to laziness and realizing -
It wasn't the lack of time that made it hard
but yet
the crushing realization
that your fear of failure
and what other people think
is stronger than your dream.

After decades on this Earth.
Humanity has
Built the pyramids.
Created the internet.
Developed vaccines.
Invented airplanes.
Finally learned
how to properly wash their hands.

Kicking yourself
for all the days
you complained about
going to your 9-5.

Lifting your glass of wine
Suddenly becomes your daily workout
Just remember
to switch hands

Stuck in patterns.
Destructive
Pulling them apart.
Painful
Tiny moments of change.
Scary
Becoming a new version of you
Worth it

A moment of silence
for everyone
celebrating a birthday
alone.

Wondering if this book of poetry
is really going to be considered poetry
or if I'm just putting words on a page
and
using
random
line breaks
to create space and suspense
because I have nothing better to do
other than to write this book
and hope you like it.
Feeling insecure
small
inadequate.

Your pet
suddenly becoming your coworker
and being envious
that they get to slack off
while you're stuck doing that report.

Being afraid
To cough
In public
In front of your family
Knowing that
Just one
Will cause internal panic

No sporting events.
Making bets
on how many
babies will be born
9 months from now.

Take a deep breath In.

Then out.

In.

Then out.

In.

Then out.

Remembering
That the breath.
Can release all
Anxiety
Fear
And uncertainty.

Introverts:
Stuck inside with so much to do!
Excitement

Extroverts:
I can't go out and do anything!
Sadness

Deciding to pray for the first time in years.

Dear Jesus,

Please grant me sanity in dealing with my family,
Enough alcohol to get through isolation
Moments of happiness within the chaos
And please tell all those Spring Breakers
That they're fucking idiots.

Thank you.

A power indescribable
Kicking up leaves
For a brief moment
Sweet orange lemonade
One thousand fireflies
Pinpricks on your neck
Rapids on the Colorado
Through you
Through you
Outward
Memories
Of brighter days.

Coming together
Out of selflessness
For the first time.
Businesses caring for communities.
Communities caring for businesses.
Exchanging love.
In a time
When it's needed most.

Sitting in the kitchen.
Sitting in the bedroom.
Sitting in the living room.
Sitting on the floor.
Sitting on the toilet.
Walking around aimlessly.
Repeat.

Finally learning how to cook.
Kind of.
Burning everything.
Sticking to simple.
Hoping your family still loves you.

Fearing for the weak
The old
The young
The compromised
Yourself
Knowing that death is inevitable for everyone
Hoping that you
And the ones you love most
Will make it through
Safe
Healthy
Strong